THE

ABRAHAM
ACCORDS

THE DIVINE DRAMA HUMAN DIPLOMACY

CAN'T COMPLETE

How the Fulfillment of an Ancient Promise Will Shatter
Alliances, Break Ancient Strongholds, and Bring a Peace
Beyond Understanding to the Middle East.

TABLE OF CONTENTS

INTRODUCTION

The Accord and The Architect

In the sleek, powerful rooms of world diplomacy, a new consensus is hardening. A plan is being drafted, votes are being counted, and a momentous decision is being set in motion for the United Nations General Assembly in September 2025. Led by nations like France, Britain, and Canada, a coalition is preparing to unilaterally recognize a Palestinian state, a move hailed in press releases as a "necessary step toward peace" and a "reward for moderation."

They are wrong.

Dead wrong.

This book argues that this move will not be a step toward peace, but a match thrown into a powder keg. It is not a reward for moderation, but a reward for terror. It is not an act of diplomacy, but an act of profound arrogance—a deliberate attempt by human hands to force a solution to a conflict that has defied all human solutions for generations. And history, scripture, and a terrifyingly precise pattern show that such actions do not go unanswered.

This book is the story of that pattern. It is the story of a divine drama unfolding in real-time, where the state of Israel acts as a prophetic clock, its hands advancing not with quiet ticks, but with the seismic shocks of global upheaval.

Tick. A world war erupts in Europe. From the judgment of that conflagration, the Balfour Declaration is born, promising a Jewish homeland.

Tock. A second, more horrific world war consumes the globe. From the ashes of the Holocaust, the unthinkable happens: the State of Israel is reborn.

The timer has not stopped. It is ticking now, louder than ever. As war once again rages in Europe with Russia's invasion of Ukraine, the pattern demands a third corresponding event. The gears of prophecy are turning. Something is about to happen in Israel.

This book will show you what that is.

We stand at a breathtaking precipice. The nations are lining up, just as the ancient prophets foretold, to make a fatal error: to divide the land of Israel. But there is another accord on the table, far older and more powerful than any document drafted in Brussels or New York. It is the original Abraham Accord—the promise of land, blessing, and purpose made by God Himself. Human diplomacy, in its pride, is attempting to overwrite a divine covenant. The results will be catastrophic for those who try, but ultimately glorious for the future of the Middle East.

For the peace that has eluded every secretary of state and every diplomat will not come from a negotiating table. It will be forged in the fire of a final, devastating conflict—a war detailed centuries in advance in the book of Ezekiel. It will be a war that finally breaks the ancient, demonic stronghold of hatred that has plagued the region since the time of Amalek. It will be a judgment that opens the eyes of the Arab world and refines the nation of Israel.

And on the other side of that fire, a peace beyond all understanding will emerge. Not a peace of fragile cease-fires and uneasy tolerance, but a true and lasting reconciliation.

The true Abraham Accord, authored by God Himself, will finally be realized.

What you are about to read is a documented account of this divine pattern. It is an indictment of nations blindly marching toward judgment. And it is a message of stunning hope—that the God of Abraham, Isaac, and Jacob is about to glorify Himself by doing what humanity could not: He will bring His children, Arabs and Jews alike, together in a peace that will stun the world.

The clock is ticking. Turn the page. Understand what is to come.

CHAPTER 1

THE FIRST STROKE OF THE PEN: BALFOUR'S PROMISE FROM THE ASHES OF EMPIRE

The world was coming apart at the seams.

It was the autumn of 1917, and the First World War—the "War to End All Wars"—was locked in a gruesome stalemate. In the trenches of the Western Front, millions of men drowned in mud and blood. The once-mighty empires of Europe—the Ottomans, the Austro-Hungarians, the Russians, and soon, the Germans—were groaning under the weight of their own pride and folly, their foundations cracking. It was a period of unprecedented, industrialized slaughter; a divine judgment, as this book will argue, on a continent that had long traded its spiritual heritage for imperial ambition.

Amid this global cataclysm, in the smoke-filled rooms of Whitehall, a solitary letter was being drafted. It was not a military stratagem for breaking the stalemate at Passchendaele. It was not a plan to shore up the crumbling Eastern Front. It was a 67-word document addressed to a private citizen, a leader of the British Jewish community. It seemed, on the surface, a trivial thing. A footnote to the vast, bloody narrative of the war.

But history would reveal it to be the first, deafening tick of the Isaiah Clock.

This letter, known to history as the Balfour Declaration, did not create the state of Israel. But it did something perhaps more profound: it planted the flag of international legitimacy for a Jewish national home in Palestine. Dated November 2, 1917, it stated:

"His Majesty's Government view with favour the establishment in Palestine of a national home for the Jewish people, and will use their best endeavours to facilitate the achievement of this object, it being clearly understood that nothing shall be done which may prejudice the civil and religious rights of existing non-Jewish communities in Palestine, or the rights and political status enjoyed by Jews in any other country."

The timing was not coincidental. It was catalytic.

Consider the geopolitical landscape. The British army was poised to break the Ottoman hold on Palestine. Just weeks after the Declaration was published, General Allenby's forces marched into Jerusalem. The 400-year-old Islamic Ottoman rule was over, defeated by a Christian power that had just promised the land to the Jewish people. This was not mere military strategy; it was the hand of history, of providence, moving pieces on a global chessboard.

But why would the world's greatest empire make such a promise at such a time? The cynical explanations are well-rehearsed: they needed Jewish support for the war effort, both in financing and in influencing the United States; they wanted a friendly power astride the Suez Canal.

While these factors played a role, they are insufficient. They explain the how, but not the why now. To understand that, one must see the larger pattern.

The war was a great breaking. It was the end of a world order. And from the broken pieces of empires judged and found wanting, a new thing was being assembled. The Balfour

Declaration was the first piece of that new mosaic. It was a divine promise, extracted from the heart of a global judgment.

Every nation that had held sway over the Jewish people—either through persecution or neglect—was being dismantled. The Ottoman Empire, which had controlled the land of Israel, was being dismembered. Czarist Russia, a hotbed of violent pogroms, had already collapsed in the Bolshevik Revolution earlier that same year. The German and Austro-Hungarian empires, centers of both Enlightenment hope and new, virulent anti-Semitism, were teetering on the brink of catastrophic defeat.

The message in the pattern is clear: When God moves to restore His people to their land, He first judges the nations that have held them captive.

The Balfour Declaration was not the fulfillment of the prophecy; it was the promise of it. It was the first stroke of the pen on the divine accord. It was a sound in the spiritual realm—a declaration that the clock of prophecy, frozen for nearly two millennia, had begun to tick again.

The nations involved in that great judgment—Britain, France, Russia—all emerged from the war shattered, their power and prestige forever diminished from their pre-war glory. They had been used as instruments to advance a divine purpose, and in the process, were themselves broken by the same forces of judgment.

The stage was now set. The promise was made. But a promise is not a nation. For that to be born, the world would need to endure a second, far greater breaking. The clock was ticking toward a horror beyond imagination, from which a nation would literally rise from the ashes.

But that is the story of the next tick. The next chapter.

CHAPTER 2

THE SECOND TICK: A NATION BORN FROM THE ASHES OF THE HOLOCAUST

If the First World War was a breaking, the Second was an annihilation.

The scale of the horror defied comprehension. Entire cities across Europe and Asia were reduced to smoldering rubble. The death toll soared into the tens of millions. And at the heart of this maelstrom of violence, a darkness so profound emerged that it would forever stain the conscience of humanity: the industrial, systematic extermination of six million Jews.

The Holocaust was not merely a war crime; it was a demonic crescendo, the ultimate expression of the ancient Amalekite spirit—the fervent, irrational desire to "blot out the remembrance of Amalek" by eradicating every Jewish man, woman, and child from the earth. It was the absolute judgment on a European continent that had, for centuries, cultivated the seeds of anti-Semitism that finally blossomed into the Final Solution.

Yet, in the perfect, terrifying symmetry of the divine pattern, it was from the absolute depths of this judgment that the next prophetic leap occurred. The second, deafening tock of the Isaiah Clock echoed from the gas chambers of Auschwitz to the voting halls of the United Nations.

The connection is as historically factual as it is theologically profound. The world emerged from the war shattered, guilty, and horrified. The evidence of the death camps, broadcast to a stunned global audience, created an undeniable moral imperative. How could the nations of the world, who had either perpetrated, enabled, or stood by as six million were slaughtered, deny the surviving remnant a sliver of safety, a sliver of sovereignty? The question answered itself in a wave of global shame and conviction.

On November 29, 1947, the United Nations—the very body created from the ashes of the war to prevent future genocide—voted on Resolution 181: the Partition Plan for Palestine. It was a direct result of the Holocaust. The nations, judged and condemned by their own inaction or complicity,

11

now felt compelled to act. They voted to divide the land, to create two states: one Arab, one Jewish.

The Jewish leadership accepted the painful compromise. The Arab world rejected it utterly, declaring immediate war to strangle the Jewish state at birth. This was the world's first glimpse of the immutable law this book seeks to expose: Human attempts to dictate terms for the Jewish homeland, especially through division, are met not with peace, but with instant, violent rejection from the forces of hatred.

Yet, the pattern held. On May 14, 1948, as the last British soldier left the soil of Palestine, David Ben-Gurion stood in a small museum in Tel Aviv and declared the establishment of the State of Israel. He read from a scroll that did not cite UN Resolution 181 as its source of legitimacy. Instead, he grounded the new state's existence in an older, more enduring promise:

"The Land of Israel was the birthplace of the Jewish people. Here their spiritual, religious and political identity was shaped. Here they first attained to statehood, created cultural values of national and universal significance and gave to the world the eternal Book of Books."

The nations of the world had voted, but they were merely ratifying a decree that had already been issued in the heavenly courts. The state was not created by the UN; it was recognized by it. Its true midwife was the providential hand of God, working through the darkest judgment in human history to bring about a stunning rebirth.

Just as with the first tick, the nations that stood in opposition were judged. The British Empire, which had reneged on the Balfour Declaration and blocked Jewish refugees from escaping the Nazis, saw its global empire evaporate almost overnight, its power broken forever. The European powers that had harbored the venom of anti-Semitism lay in ruins, physically and morally. And the nations that immediately moved to war against the infant state of Israel—Egypt, Jordan, Syria, Iraq—were soundly defeated by a tiny population of survivors who fought with the desperate strength of those who had nowhere left to run.

The pattern was now unmistakably clear:

1. Global Cataclysm (Judgment on the Nations): World War I -> World War II.

2. Prophetic Advancement for Israel: Balfour Declaration (Promise of a Home) -> Birth of the Nation (Fulfillment of the Promise).

A promise had become a reality. The clock had advanced. But the peace did not come. The ancient stronghold was not broken; it had merely shifted its address. It dug into the refugee camps, festered in the halls of Arab dictators, and fomented a new, relentless war of attrition and terror against the Jewish state.

For seventy-five years, Israel has known nothing but conflict. Because the final stronghold—the spiritual one—remained. And as history and this pattern show, it would take a third, and final, global upheaval to break it.

The timer is counting down. The world is once again at war in Europe. The nations are once again preparing to divide the land. The pattern demands a conclusion.

The third tick is imminent.

CHAPTER 3

THE UNCEASING TIMER: THE ANCIENT STRONGHOLD AGAINST ZION

For seventy-five years, the nation-state of Israel has stood. For seventy-five years, it has known not a single day of genuine, comprehensive peace. This is not a political anomaly. It is a spiritual fact.

To understand the relentless nature of the conflict—the endless rounds of war, terrorism, and diplomatic persecution—one must look beyond politics, beyond resources, beyond borders. One must journey back to the arid wastes of the Sinai Peninsula, to the very dawn of Israel's national existence, to encounter the first and most venomous enemy they ever faced: Amalek.

The story is recorded in the ancient text of Exodus. Fresh from the miraculous Red Sea deliverance, a vulnerable and weary Israel is trekking through the desert. They are not attacking anyone. They are not conquering any land. They are simply trying to survive their journey. It is at this moment of vulnerability that Amalek attacks (Exodus 17:8-16).

This attack is the prototype, the original spiritual DNA, for all subsequent hatred against the Jewish people. Its characteristics are chillingly familiar:

1. Irrational Hatred: Amalek had no territorial dispute with Israel. They were not defending their borders. Their attack was motivated by pure, unadulterated malice.

2. Targeting the Weak: The Talmud explains Amalek's tactic: they "cooled the bath" for the nations of the world. After the miracles of the Red Sea, the nations were terrified of Israel. Amalek showed they were vulnerable by attacking the stragglers—the tired, the weak, the elderly at the rear of the camp. They specialize in attacking the defenseless.

3. A Cosmic Battle: Moses understood this was no ordinary fight. As Joshua battled in the valley, Moses stood on a hill, his raised hands determining the outcome. The battle was not won by military prowess alone; it was won through intercession. It was a spiritual war.

God's response to Amalek is stark and eternal: "I will completely blot out the name of Amalek from under heaven."

And later, "The Lord will be at war against Amalek from generation to generation" (Exodus 17:14, 16).

This is not a historical footnote. It is a divine indictment against a specific spirit of evil. And that spirit did not die in the desert. It has manifested itself in every generation, in every empire, and in every ideology that has ever sought the eradication of the Jewish people.

Haman, in the book of Esther, who plotted to annihilate all the Jews in the Persian Empire, is called an Agagite—a descendant of Agag, king of the Amalekites.

The Nazis perfected the Amalekite strategy: irrational hatred combined with the industrial-scale targeting of the weak and defenseless in gas chambers and concentration camps.

The Soviet Union institutionalized it through the Doctors' Plot and state-sponsored anti-Zionism, seeking to blot out Jewish identity.

And today, this ancient stronghold operates openly in the Middle East. It is not merely a political position; it is a genocidal mandate.

Hamas: The governing authority in Gaza. Its founding charter is a modern Amalekite manifesto. It quotes the hadith about stones and trees betraying Jews so they can be killed (a call for total genocide). It rejects any negotiation or peace process. It specializes in Amalek's signature tactic: targeting the defenseless, using its own civilians as human shields while launching rockets at Israeli civilian centers.

Hezbollah: The Iranian proxy in Lebanon. Its stated purpose, as declared by its Secretary-General, is the elimination of the "Zionist entity."

The Regime in Iran: The central banker of modern Amalekism. Its leaders routinely deny the Holocaust while promising to enact a new one. They openly call for Israel to be wiped off the map, financing and arming proxies on every border to achieve this goal.

This is why all human peace processes have failed. This is why the "Two-State Solution" is a perpetual fantasy when discussed in secular diplomatic terms. You cannot sign a treaty with a spirit. You cannot negotiate a land swap with a demonic stronghold whose only demand is your non-existence.

The "peace" offered by these entities is not peace. It is merely a hudna—a temporary Islamic ceasefire—to be broken when they are strong enough to resume their genocidal war. This is why every Israeli withdrawal, from Lebanon to Gaza, has been met not with peace, but with an exponential increase in attacks. To feed the stronghold with more land is to feed a fire with gasoline.

The timer of conflict has not ceased because the stronghold has not been broken. The world, in its secular myopia, diagnoses a political dispute and prescribes political solutions. But you do not treat a metastatic cancer with a band-aid.

The pattern of global judgment and prophetic advancement we have established—the ticking of the Isaiah Clock—demands a final, corresponding event. The first two ticks advanced Israel's physical restoration. The third must deal with its spiritual security. It must finally break the ancient stronghold of Amalek.

This is why the coming conflict, foretold by Ezekiel, is inevitable. It is not a war Israel seeks, but a war that the spirit of Amalek, festering in Tehran, Gaza, and Beirut, is relentlessly provoking. It will be a war unlike any other, because its ultimate objective will be not merely to win a battle, but to break a curse. It will be the judgment through which God Himself finally blots out the name of Amalek from the modern world and secures the peace that has eluded humanity for millennia.

The nations, ignorant of this spiritual reality, are now lining up to make a catastrophic error. They are preparing to reward this Amalekite spirit with statehood. In doing so, they are not promoting peace. They are signing a covenant with death.

And as the next chapter will show, when nations align themselves with this ancient stronghold, they inevitably find themselves on the wrong side of history, and of judgment.

CHAPTER 4

THE THIRD SIGNATORY: WAR IN EUROPE AND THE UNFOLDING PROPHETIC ALIGNMENT

A shadow has once again fallen across Europe. For the first time since the horrors of the Second World War, the continent is witnessing the brutal, large-scale invasion of one nation by another. On February 24, 2022, Russian tanks rolled across the border into Ukraine, unleashing a storm of fire, death, and a refugee crisis that has destabilized the global order.

The world's attention snapped to the latest crisis. News cycles became saturated with images of destroyed cities in Mariupol and Bakhmut. Diplomats scrambled. Sanctions regimes were hastily assembled. Billions in aid were pledged. For the Western world, Ukraine became the central front—the battle for democracy, for the "rules-based international order," against authoritarian aggression.

But what if they are missing the bigger picture? What if this conflict, for all its immediate tragedy and geopolitical importance, is not the main event, but the backdrop? What if it is the third, decisive tick of the Isaiah Clock, setting the stage for the final act in the divine drama of Israel's restoration?

The pattern, established over a century, is impeccable and demands we ask this question:

· Global Upheaval I (World War I): The judgment on the Ottoman and European empires -> The Balfour Declaration (The Promise of a Home).

· Global Upheaval II (World War II): The judgment on Nazi Germany and the West -> The Birth of the Nation of Israel (The Fulfillment of the Promise).

· Global Upheaval III (The Ukraine War): The judgment on Russia and the weakening of the West -> ???

The correlation is not merely thematic; it is causal. The world's focus and resources are being dramatically diverted. The United States, the traditional guarantor of Middle East security and the primary broker of the Abraham Accords, is stretched thin, its military and diplomatic attention divided between Asia, Europe, and the Middle East. Europe, addicted to Russian energy and now facing a massive security and refugee crisis, is inwardly focused and weakened.

This creates a power vacuum. And into every vacuum in the Middle East, a force always moves: the Islamic Republic of Iran and its proxies, empowered by their alliance with a resurgent Russia.

While the world watches Ukraine, the eyes of Tehran, Moscow, Beijing, and the terrorist proxies are fixed on Israel. They see a moment of unprecedented opportunity. They perceive a distracted and divided West, an America led by a administration perceived as hesitant, and a Israel that appears more isolated than ever on the global stage. This is the perfect storm for which the spirit of Amalek has been waiting.

Russia's involvement is the key connector. It is the nation at the heart of the European upheaval, and it is also the primary patron and protector of the Amalekite regime in Iran. It provides the diplomatic cover at the UN, the advanced military technology, and the economic lifeline that allows Iran to survive crippling sanctions and continue funding its terrorist armies on Israel's borders—Hezbollah in Lebanon, Hamas and Islamic Jihad in Gaza, and proxies in Syria.

The war in Ukraine has not created a new reality; it has accelerated an existing one. It has brought the emerging axis of evil—Moscow, Tehran, Beijing—into sharp relief. This axis is united by a common goal: to dismantle the American-led world order. And the central obstacle to their regional dominance in the Middle East is the State of Israel.

Therefore, the Ukraine conflict is the third global signatory on the divine scroll. It is the event that is creating the precise conditions foretold by the prophet Ezekiel:

A Distracted World: "Sheba and Dedan and the merchants of Tarshish and all her villages [often interpreted as Western powers] will say to you, 'Have you come to plunder? Have you gathered your hordes to loot, to carry off silver and gold, to take away livestock and goods and to seize much plunder?'" (Ezekiel 38:13). The West will protest, but will they act? The pattern suggests they will be too preoccupied, too weakened.

An Emboldened Foe: Russia's role is provocatively aligned with that of "Gog, of the land of Magog, the chief prince of Meshech and Tubal" (Ezekiel 38:2-3), the northern power that leads a multinational coalition against a restored Israel "living in safety" (Ezekiel 38:8, 11).

A Multi-Front Coalition: The Ezekiel coalition includes Persia (modern-day Iran), Put (likely Libya), and Cush (often associated with Sudan). This is not a historical anomaly; it is a current events headline. Iran's proxies now encircle Israel.

The timer is sounding. The conditions are being met. The Third Signatory—the war in Ukraine—is creating the chaos and distraction necessary for the ancient prophecy to find its modern fulfillment.

While diplomats in Paris, London, and Ottawa draft their plans for a September 2025 vote to recognize Palestine, believing they are crafting peace, they are profoundly mistaken. They are not reading the signs. They are not hearing the clock. They are attempting to build a house of cards on the epicenter of an earthquake.

Their planned vote is not a peace initiative. It is the spark that will ignite the tinderbox that the Ukraine war has helped stack around Israel. It will be interpreted by the forces of Amalek not as a gesture of peace, but as a sign of Israel's ultimate abandonment by the West. It will signal that the time for their final offensive is now.

The world is fixated on the conflict in Europe, but the next great earthquake will originate in the Middle East. The pattern is real. The third tick has occurred.

The storm is now inevitable.

CHAPTER 5

THE SEPTEMBER ULTIMATUM: A DIPLOMATIC DECLARATION OF WAR AND THE COMING JUDGMENT

In the halls of power in Paris, London, and Ottawa, a dangerous and arrogant consensus is coalescing. Under the banner of peace and a twisted sense of justice, a coalition of nations is preparing for a momentous act at the United Nations General Assembly in September 2025: the unilateral recognition of a Palestinian state.

They will frame this act as a courageous step toward a Two-State Solution. They will posture as champions of human rights and defenders of the oppressed. They will use the language of diplomacy to mask a profound spiritual rebellion.

This chapter serves as a direct indictment and a solemn warning to France, Britain, and Canada: Your planned vote is not a path to peace. It is a declaration of war against divine order. It is an attempt to force a human solution onto a spiritual problem, and history shows that such arrogance invites severe judgment.

This is not speculation; it is the immutable pattern of history and scripture. The prophet Joel delivers a chilling decree from the Lord concerning the latter days: "I will gather all nations and bring them down to the Valley of Jehoshaphat. There I will put them on trial for what they have done to my inheritance, my people Israel, because they scattered my people among the nations and divided up my land" (Joel 3:2, emphasis added).

The nations planning this vote are not ignorant of this warning; they are indifferent to it. They are poised to commit the exact transgression Joel prophesied: they are moving to divide the land of Israel.

Let us examine the defendants in this indictment:

1. France: A nation that has long fancied itself a counterweight to American influence in the Middle East. This move is not about peace; it is about reclaiming a relevance it lost decades ago. It is a nation that has

struggled with its own internal demons of anti-Semitism, now projecting its failed multicultural policies onto the world stage by legitimizing a regime whose founding charter is genocidal.

2. Britain: The most culpable, and therefore, the most condemned. This is the nation that issued the Balfour Declaration—a sacred promise to the Jewish people. It is the nation that later betrayed that promise with the White Papers, blocking Jewish refugees from escaping the Nazi death camps. Now, a century after its first momentous decision, it seeks to complete its betrayal by presiding over the dismemberment of the very state it helped midwife. It is a tragic cycle of promise and perfidy.

3. Canada: Once a steadfast friend of Israel, it now abandons its principles for a seat on the global stage. Under the guise of "progressivism," it is sacrificing a longstanding ally on the altar of political correctness and oil interests, betraying its own history of moral clarity for a vague and dangerous multilateralism.

Their action is based on a catastrophic misdiagnosis. They believe the conflict is about borders and settlements. It is not. It is about the ancient stronghold of Amalek—the irreconcilable hatred that denies Israel's right to exist at all.

By granting unilateral recognition, these nations are doing the following:

· Rewarding Terrorism: They are telling Hamas, Islamic Jihad, and the Palestinian Authority that decades of murderous terror, intifadas, and rocket attacks are effective. The message is clear: reject peace, murder Jews, and eventually the international community will force Israel to give you what you want.

· Sabotaging Real Negotiations: Why would any Palestinian leader ever again sit down to negotiate difficult compromises—on Jerusalem, on refugees, on security—if they can simply wait for European nations to hand them a state without requiring them to concede anything, even the right to wage war?

· Legitimizing a Terror State: They are not creating a state for peace; they are creating a terror state, a Hamasstan, on the doorstep of Israel's financial and population centers. They are gifting Iran another military front.

But beyond the geopolitical foolishness lies the true danger: the invocation of divine judgment. The pattern is clear.

Nations that have sought to divide the land of Israel or curse the Jewish people have faced historic consequences.

Great Britain: Issued the Balfour Declaration but later betrayed it. Result? The sun set on the British Empire within a generation.

The Soviet Union: Led the global campaign of anti-Zionism. Result? Collapsed and ceased to exist.

Iraq: Fired Scud missiles at Israel in 1991. Result? Defeated and its leader toppled.

Spain: Expelled its Jewish population in 1492. Result? Its golden age ended, and it faded from global prominence.

France, Britain, and Canada are now lining up to add their names to this list. Their vote in September 2025 will be the modern equivalent of drawing a line through the heart of Israel on a map. They believe they are drawing a border; in reality, they are signing their own subpoena to stand in the Valley of Jehoshaphat.

This act will be the catalyst. It will embolden the Psalm 83 coalition beyond measure. They will see the West's abandonment of Israel as a green light for their long-planned war of annihilation. The September vote will not bring peace; it will ignite the firestorm.

It is an ultimatum—not to Israel, but to God Himself. And the response will be according to the pattern He has established throughout history. The nations are warned. The case is presented. The judgment, should they proceed, is inevitable.

CHAPTER 6

THE EZEKIEL CATALYST: THE FIRE THAT FORGES THE FINAL PEACE

Humanity stands on the brink of its most cherished ideal and most elusive dream: peace in the Middle East. Yet the path to that peace, as revealed through the unchangeable pattern of history and scripture, does not run through air-conditioned conference rooms in Geneva or New York. It runs through the valley of judgment. It is forged in the fire of a conflict so devastating, so conclusive, that it will finally shatter the ancient stronghold of Amalek that has held the region captive for millennia.

This coming conflict is not a vague prediction; it is a detailed prophecy, recorded over 2,500 years ago. It is the master key to understanding the next—and final—phase of the Isaiah Clock. While the nations conspire to divide the land in September 2025, God has already declared His plan to unite His people in ultimate security.

The prophet Ezekiel, speaking to a people in exile, delivered a message of stunning hope and sobering clarity. He foretold a specific war and its even more specific outcome:

"This is what the Sovereign Lord says: I will gather you from the nations and bring you back from the countries where you have been scattered, and I will give you back the land of Israel again... And they will live there in safety... Then they will know that I am the Lord their God, for though I sent them into exile among the nations, I will gather them to their own land, not leaving any behind... I will no longer hide my face from them, for I will pour out my Spirit on the people of Israel, declares the Sovereign Lord." (Ezekiel 28:25-26, excerpts)

This is the divine promise. But the promise is preceded by a purging. Just a few verses earlier, the prophecy outlines the mechanism:

"I will execute judgment upon him [the hostile nations]... I will inflict punishment on him... and he will be turned over to the sword... I will send a sword upon him... and I will make

him a ruin... Then they will know that I am the Lord."
(Ezekiel 28:22-23, paraphrased)

This is the Ezekiel Catalyst. It is the war that must come before the peace can dawn.

The coalition Ezekiel describes is not the distant army of Gog from the north (a later event in chapters 38-39). This is a judgment on the nations that are "round about" Israel (Ezekiel 28:24, KJV)—the immediate neighbors, the Psalm 83 conspirators. This is a regional war for regional purification.

The modern alignment is unmistakable. The "nations round about" form a perfect ring of fire around the Jewish state:

Gaza (Philistia) – Hamas and Palestinian Islamic Jihad.

Lebanon (Tyre) – Hezbollah, the world's most heavily armed non-state terrorist army.

Syria – A failed state hosting Iranian Revolutionary Guard Corps bases and proxies.

Jordan (Ammon, Moab, Edom) – While officially at peace, its population seethes with hatred, and it serves as a base for terrorist activities.

Saudi Arabia & The Gulf States (Ishmaelites, Dedan) – Financiers of the global jihadist movement, whose ideological hatred fuels the conflict, even if their governments temporarily hedge their bets.

Iran (Persia) – The puppet master, the spiritual and financial heart of the modern Amalekite empire.

This is the coalition that will move, emboldened by the West's distraction over Ukraine and its perceived betrayal of Israel at the UN in September 2025. They will see their moment and attack, believing they can finally achieve their genocidal goal.

But they will have miscalculated catastrophically. They will have moved not against a mere nation, but against the covenant people of the Living God. And they will have walked directly into the precise scenario Ezekiel outlined.

The war will be horrific. It will be a multi-front conflict of a scale and intensity Israel has never faced. Rockets will darken skies. Cities will be threatened. The world will watch in horror, and many will blame Israel for defending itself.

But the outcome is not in doubt. The prophecy is clear: Israel will be victorious. Not by its own strength alone, but by the hand of God Himself, intervening as He did in the days of Moses on the hilltop. This will be a victory so decisive, so disproportionate, that no human general or army can claim the credit.

This is the catalyst. The Ezekiel war will achieve what 75 years of diplomacy could not:

1. It Will Break the Military Power of the Amalekite Coalition: Hamas, Hezbollah, and the IRGC's infrastructure in Syria will be utterly dismantled. Their ability to make war will be obliterated for a generation.

2. It Will Shatter the Spiritual Stronghold of Hatred: The ideology of annihilation will be discredited on the battlefield. When the people of the region see their invincible champions decisively and miraculously defeated, the veil will begin to lift. The lie that Israel can be destroyed will be broken.

3. It Will Force a Divine Recognition: "Then they will know that I am the Lord." This is the ultimate goal. The defeat will be so profound that it will force a spiritual reckoning. It will open eyes to see that the God of Israel is not a regional deity, but the Sovereign Lord of history.

The September vote at the UN is man's futile attempt to create peace by decree. The Ezekiel Catalyst is God's proven method of establishing peace through righteous judgment. One will lead to fire; the other will lead through the fire to the only peace that can truly last.

The stage is set. The players are in place. The catalyst is ready to be activated. The firestorm is coming, and from its ashes, the Phoenix of true peace will finally rise.

CHAPTER 7

THE BREAKER OF STRONGHOLDS: HOW JUDGMENT PAVES THE WAY FOR GRACE

The dust settles over the mountains of Judea and Samaria. The acrid smell of smoke and spent munitions hangs heavy in the air. The constant, deafening roar of jets, the percussive thump of artillery, the wail of sirens—all have fallen silent. An eerie, unfamiliar quiet descends upon the land of Israel.

The war is over.

The Ezekiel Catalyst has achieved its terrifying, purifying purpose. The military might of the "nations round about"— the Hamas regime in Gaza, the Hezbollah state-within-a-state in Lebanon, the Iranian terror infrastructure in Syria—lies in utter ruins. Their command structures are decimated, their vast arsenals of rockets and tunnels destroyed, their ability to threaten the Jewish state extinguished for a generation.

But the true victory was not won on the physical battlefield. The true victory occurred in the spiritual realm. The ancient, suffocating stronghold of Amalek—the spirit of irrational, genocidal hatred that has fueled this conflict for generations—has been broken.

For decades, this stronghold had built walls around the hearts and minds of millions. It was fed by state-sponsored propaganda that taught children to venerate martyrdom. It was enforced by terrorist regimes that punished moderation with death. It was sustained by a theology of victimhood that blamed every ailment on the "Zionist entity." It was a spiritual prison, and its gates were locked from the inside.

The Ezekiel war did not just defeat armies; it shattered the very foundations of that prison.

How?

The victory was too complete. Too miraculous. Too unnatural. The nations of the world, watching the conflict unfold, saw a small nation, surrounded on all sides by enemies sworn to its destruction, not only survive but achieve a victory so decisive it defied all military logic. The intelligence was preternatural. The coordination between branches of the Israeli Defense Forces was flawless. Enemy weapons failed. Their strategies collapsed into confusion.

To the secular world, it will be a stunning military feat. But to the people of the region—to the Arab street, to the ordinary citizen in Cairo, in Amman, in Riyadh—a deeper truth will begin to dawn. They will recall the stories from their grandparents of the wars in 1948, 1967, and 1973, when the same inexplicable phenomenon occurred. They will remember the ancient texts they were taught to dismiss.

They will begin to ask the forbidden question: "What if the God of Israel is real?"

This is the great eye-opening. This is the moment the stronghold cracks.

The old lies will collapse under the weight of their own absurdity. How can Israel be both an omnipotent, global evil and a tiny nation desperately fighting for its survival? How can it be a Nazi-like regime and the only country in the region that grants freedom of worship to all faiths? The cognitive dissonance, held in place for decades by the stronghold of hatred, will become unbearable.

The defeat of their champions will create a vacuum—not of power, but of ideology. The fiery imams and hate-spewing dictators will be discredited. Their promise of victory through jihad has led only to ash and ruin. Their followers will feel a profound sense of betrayal.

And into this vacuum, truth will begin to flow.

People will start to seek answers elsewhere. They will find satellite channels and internet sites (no longer blocked by terrorist regimes) showing a different Israel. They will see the Israeli doctors who treated Syrian civilians during their civil war. They will see the Israeli agricultural technology that could feed their own nations. They will see a vibrant, creative democracy.

Most importantly, they will see the Jewish people not as the cartoonish demons of propaganda, but as a people who simply longed for 2,000 years to return to their ancestral home, who have been forced to become warriors to protect their children from fire, and who have now been delivered by a hand far mightier than their own.

This is the judgment that leads to grace. The fire that burns away the dross to reveal the pure metal beneath. God is not judging the people of the Middle East; He is judging the spirit that has held them captive. He is breaking the chains of hatred so that His love can finally reach them.

The stronghold of Amalek is built on a lie: that God hates the Jewish people and that their eradication is a holy act. The aftermath of the Ezekiel Catalyst will prove the opposite: that God has fiercely protected His people and that His covenant with them is eternal. His judgment on the nations was not against Arabs or Muslims, but against the demonic power that deceived them.

The eyes of the Arab world will be opened not to a new political reality, but to a divine one. They will see that the God of Abraham, Isaac, and Jacob is the one true God. That He loves them as much as He loves the Jews. That His desire is not their destruction, but their salvation. That the true enemy was never the Jew in Tel Aviv, but the spirit of hatred in their own hearts, now finally broken.

The path will now be clear. The obstacle removed. The stage is set not for a tense ceasefire, but for a genuine reconciliation. The peace that follows will not be built on the fragile foundation of human diplomacy, but on the unshakable foundation of divine revelation.

The Breaker has gone up before them. The stronghold is fallen. Now, the healing can begin.

CHAPTER 8

THE GREAT UNVEILING: WHEN EYES ARE OPENED AND HEARTS ARE UNLOCKED

In the silence that follows the storm, a sound emerges that has not been heard in the Middle East for generations, perhaps centuries. It is not the sound of a truce being negotiated, nor the hesitant scratching of pens on a peace treaty. It is the sound of a key turning in a long-locked door. It is the sound of a veil, woven from lies and hatred, being torn in two.

This is The Great Unveiling. It is the moment the spiritual scales fall from the eyes of the Arab world, and they see—truly see—their Jewish neighbors for the first time.

The Ezekiel Catalyst has done its work. The military threat is neutralized. But the true miracle is not the silence of the rockets; it is the silencing of the poison that flowed from pulpits, media, and textbooks. The infrastructure of hatred lies in ruins, and without its constant reinforcement, the old narrative cannot hold. A new reality, one that was always there but hidden from view, is suddenly, blindingly obvious.

Imagine the scene:

In a café in Dubai, a young Emirati man, raised on a diet of anti-Israeli vitriol, watches a documentary on his phone. He sees footage of the recent war: an Israeli pilot, ordered to destroy a Hezbollah rocket launcher, aborting his strike at the last second because he sees children being used as human shields nearby. The pilot's frustration, his humanity, is palpable. The young man sits back, stunned. This is the " Zionist monster"?

In a university in Jordan, a history professor, her previous lectures filled with the tropes of colonialist Israel, now assigns a new text: the history of the ancient Israelites, their connection to Jerusalem, their exile, and their longing to return. She teaches not propaganda, but truth. The students, freed from the obligation to hate, are fascinated. They begin to ask, "Why were we never told this?"

In a village once controlled by Hamas, an elderly Palestinian man watches an Israeli medical unit set up a makeshift clinic to treat the wounded—both Arab and Jew. He remembers the Hamas leaders who stole aid money, built tunnels instead of schools, and hid behind their own people. He looks at the Israeli doctors and weeps. The clarity is painful, and liberating.

This is the fulfillment of the prophecy: "Then they will know that I am the LORD."

This knowing is not intellectual assent. It is a deep, heart-level revelation. It is the sudden understanding that the God of the Bible is real and that He has been moving in history all along. It is the realization that they have been fighting not just the Jews, but the God of the Jews. And in losing that fight, they have been freed from a terrible deception.

The change is not orchestrated by governments or NGOs. It is organic, bubbling up from the people. It is a grassroots movement of remorse, curiosity, and a desperate hunger for truth.

And how does Israel respond? Not with triumphalism, but with tears of its own. After generations of living in a fortress mentality, of seeing every Arab face as a potential threat, the Israeli people witness this awakening with awe. The walls around their own hearts begin to crumble. The fear and suspicion that were necessary for survival begin to dissolve, replaced by a cautious, then joyous, embrace.

The Jewish people, understanding their divine mandate to be a "light to the nations" (Isaiah 42:6), step into their role as healers and restorers. Israeli agronomists are invited to Egypt to help with water desalination. Israeli cybersecurity experts partner with Gulf states to create a safer region. Israeli musicians hold joint concerts with Palestinian artists in Jericho.

The reconciliation is not a denial of the past, but a transcendence of it. It is acknowledged that great wrongs were committed on all sides. But the spirit of Amalek, the father of those wrongs, has been judged and broken. A new spirit is moving—the Spirit of the God of Abraham, who loves both Ishmael and Isaac.

This is the true Abraham Accord. It was never meant to be signed in a foreign embassy. It is being signed in shared business ventures, in collaborative scientific research, in interfaith dialogues where Imams and Rabbis study the Torah and Quran together, discovering their shared father and their shared values.

The peace that emerges is not the cold peace of diplomats. It is a warm peace of cousins reunited. It is the peace of a family that, after a long and bitter feud, finally remembers its common bloodline. It is the peace that passes all understanding because its architect is not man, but God.

The nations of the world, particularly those in Europe and North America who prophesied doom and pushed for division, look on in stunned silence. Their cynical realpolitik, their arrogant attempts to force a solution, lie in the ash heap of history. They are revealed to have been not peacemakers, but obstacles to the divine plan.

The Great Unveiling reveals the ultimate truth: God loves the Arab people. He never desired their destruction, only their liberation from the father of lies. He judged the stronghold not to punish them, but to free them. And in freeing them, He has now glorified Himself before all the nations of the earth, demonstrating His power, His mercy, and His unfathomable love for all the children of Abraham.

The eyes of the blind have been opened. The hearts of the estranged have been unlocked. The unveiling is complete. Now, the future can begin.

CONCLUSION

THE CHOICE BEFORE THE NATIONS

We began this investigation at the edge of a precipice, with the nations of the world assembling to make a fateful decision. We end it with a clear-eyed vision of the two paths that lie before them—and before us all.

The evidence has been presented. The pattern is irrefutable. For over a century, the Isaiah Clock has advanced not in times of quiet, but in the roaring furnaces of global judgment. World War I gave us the promise of a Jewish home. World War II gave us the reality of a Jewish state. Now, the third great conflagration—the war in Ukraine—has sounded the timer's most urgent toll, setting the stage for the final act: the war that will break the ancient curse and bring the peace that has eluded all human effort.

This is not a message of doom. It is a message of ultimate hope, but one that passes through the refining fire of truth.

The nations led by France, Britain, and Canada now stand at a historic crossroads. The path they are currently on—the path toward unilateral recognition of a Palestinian state in September 2025—is a path of profound arrogance. It is the belief that human wisdom can untie a Gordian knot that God Himself, through the prophet Joel, said would bring the nations into judgment. It is a path that rewards terrorism, empowers the spirit of Amalek, and ignites the very firestorm it claims to want to prevent. To choose this path is to willfully ignore the lessons of the last hundred years. It is to sign your own nation's subpoena to stand in the Valley of Jehoshaphat.

But there is another path.

It is the path of humility. It is the path of recognizing that the God of history is actively fulfilling His promises and that His pattern is clear. It is the path of standing aside—or better yet, standing with—what He is doing, rather than standing in opposition. It is the path of blessing, not cursing. It is the path that leads to life.

The coming Psalm 83 conflict, the Ezekiel Catalyst, is inevitable. The ancient stronghold must be broken. But nations can choose whether they will be victims of the ensuing judgment or witnesses to the ensuing miracle.

The message of this book is that true, lasting, miraculous peace is coming to the Middle East. It will not be manufactured in the United Nations. It will be forged in the aftermath of a divine judgment so decisive that it will open blind eyes and unlock hardened hearts. It will be a peace between Arabs and Jews so profound that it will stun the world, a peace that can only be explained by the direct intervention of the God of Abraham.

This is the true Abraham Accord. It was never meant to be a temporary diplomatic understanding. It is an eternal covenant of reconciliation, authored by God Himself, who loves both Isaac and Ishmael and who longs to gather all His children together.

The choice before every leader, every nation, and every reader is this: Will you see the world through the myopic lens of secular politics, or will you see it through the clear lens of prophetic history? Will you align with the fleeting consensus of men, or with the eternal decree of God?

The clock is not stopping. The hands are moving. The Third Signatory has been written. The firestorm is on the horizon, but on the other side of it lies a dawn brighter than any the region has ever known.

A time is coming, and is now very near, when Israel will dwell in safety, secure from all her enemies. The ancient stronghold will be a memory. The sound of war will be a lesson in history books. And the children of Abraham—Arabs and Jews alike—will finally live as the family they were always meant to be, a testament to the world of the power, the mercy, and the unfathomable love of the God who keeps His promises.

The pattern is real. The warning is issued. The hope is assured.

The choice is yours.

AFTERWORD

The Storm Before the Silence: Why This War is an Act of GRACE.

For the skeptic, the critic, and even the fearful believer, the thesis of this book can be a difficult pill to swallow. The notion of a coming war, no matter how prophetically sound, seems to clash with the image of a God of love. The idea that judgment precedes restoration feels archaic, harsh.

If you have found yourself wrestling with these concepts, this chapter is for you. It is designed to address the hardest questions head-on and to reveal the stunning thread of grace that runs through every moment of coming judgment.

The Unmistakable Pattern: Europe's Breaking, Israel's Becoming

Before we can look forward, we must once again look back—not with a glance, but with a studied gaze. The pattern is not a superficial coincidence; it is a deep, structural rhythm in modern history.

The First Breaking: World War I (1914-1918) The ancient empires of Europe—the Ottoman,the Austro-Hungarian, the German, and the Russian—engaged in a suicide pact. The continent that had crowned itself the pinnacle of civilization descended into barbarism in the mud of the trenches. Millions died. Old world orders crumbled. It was a divine judgment on a system that had rejected its foundation.

· Israel's Advancement: From the very heart of this cataclysm, from the government of the world's foremost empire, came the Balfour Declaration. A promise was extracted from the chaos: a national home for the Jewish people in Palestine. The hand of the clock moved from exile to promise.

The Second Breaking: World War II & The Holocaust (1939-1945) If the first war was a breaking,the second was an annihilation. The scale of evil reached its demonic zenith in the industrialized murder of the Holocaust. The world saw the ultimate fruit of the ancient Amalekite spirit and was rightly horrified. Europe, the center of this evil, was left physically and morally in ruins.

· Israel's Advancement: From the ashes of the crematoria, the international community, convicted by its own complicity and guilt, voted for the establishment of a Jewish state. On May 14, 1948, the prophecy of Isaiah 66:8 was fulfilled before a stunned world: "Who has ever heard of such things? Who has ever seen things like this? Can a country be born in a day or a nation be brought forth in a moment?" The hand of the clock moved from promise to nationhood.

The pattern is undeniable. Global upheaval, centered in Europe, leads directly to a monumental leap forward for Israel. The Ukraine War is the Third Breaking. It signals another monumental leap is imminent.

Not Annihilation, But Open Eyes: The War as Severe Mercy

This is the hardest concept to grasp: the coming war is not an act of divine annihilation, but an act of severe mercy. It is the surgical removal of a cancerous ideology that has poisoned the Middle East for generations.

God's heart is not for the destruction of the Arab people. His heart is for their liberation. The Arab world is held captive by a powerful stronghold—a spirit of hatred that distorts truth, fuels violence, and perpetuates suffering. This spirit uses human beings as pawns, teaching children to hate and promising glory in death.

How does a loving God break such a powerful deception? How does He free people who don't know they are captives?

Sometimes, He must break the system that enforces the deception. He must allow the ideology to run its full, violent course and reveal its true, bankrupt nature for all to see. The coming war will be the final, tragic exhibition of the Amalekite spirit's goals: genocide and death. And its utter, miraculous failure will be its undoing.

This defeat is designed not to crush people, but to open their eyes. When the armies, the rockets, and the hateful rhetoric fail—when the Jewish state stands victorious not by its own might but by the hand of God—the veil will lift. The people of the region will see that the God of Israel is real and that the path of hatred is a dead end. This is the ultimate act of grace: using judgment to shatter a prison of lies so that truth and reconciliation can finally enter.

A Plea to the Skeptic: Engage Before You Judge

To the critic who finds this narrative too neat, too confrontational, or too dramatic, I issue a sincere challenge: Engage with the pattern before you dismiss it.

Do not cast judgment on this thesis based on a headline or an excerpt. Read the full historical account laid out in this book. Trace the line from the assassination in Sarajevo to the Balfour Declaration. Follow the thread from the gates of Auschwitz to the voting hall of the UN. Look at the map of Ukraine today and ask yourself, with intellectual honesty: if the pattern holds, what does it mean for the epicenter of biblical prophecy?

This is not a call to blind faith. It is a call to rigorous, historical investigation. The evidence is not hidden in obscure codes; it is written in the blood and ink of 20th-century history. The Isaiah Clock is not a metaphor for doom-mongering; it is a framework for understanding how God sovereignly uses the chaos of human rebellion to advance His redemptive purposes.

Peace is coming to the Middle East. Not a fragile peace signed by politicians, but a true peace born in the hearts of people liberated from hatred. It will be a peace between cousins, a reconciliation within the family of Abraham. It will be the peace that only God Himself can give.

The storm is on the horizon. But on the other side of it is a silence more profound than anyone living has ever known. It is the silence of rockets that will never again fly, of bombs that will never again detonate, and of hateful rhetoric that has finally been exposed and rejected.

It is the silence of perfect peace. And it is worth everything it takes to get there.

www.ingramcontent.com/pod-product-compliance
Lightning Source LLC
Chambersburg PA
CBHW071348130626
46556CB00005B/2089